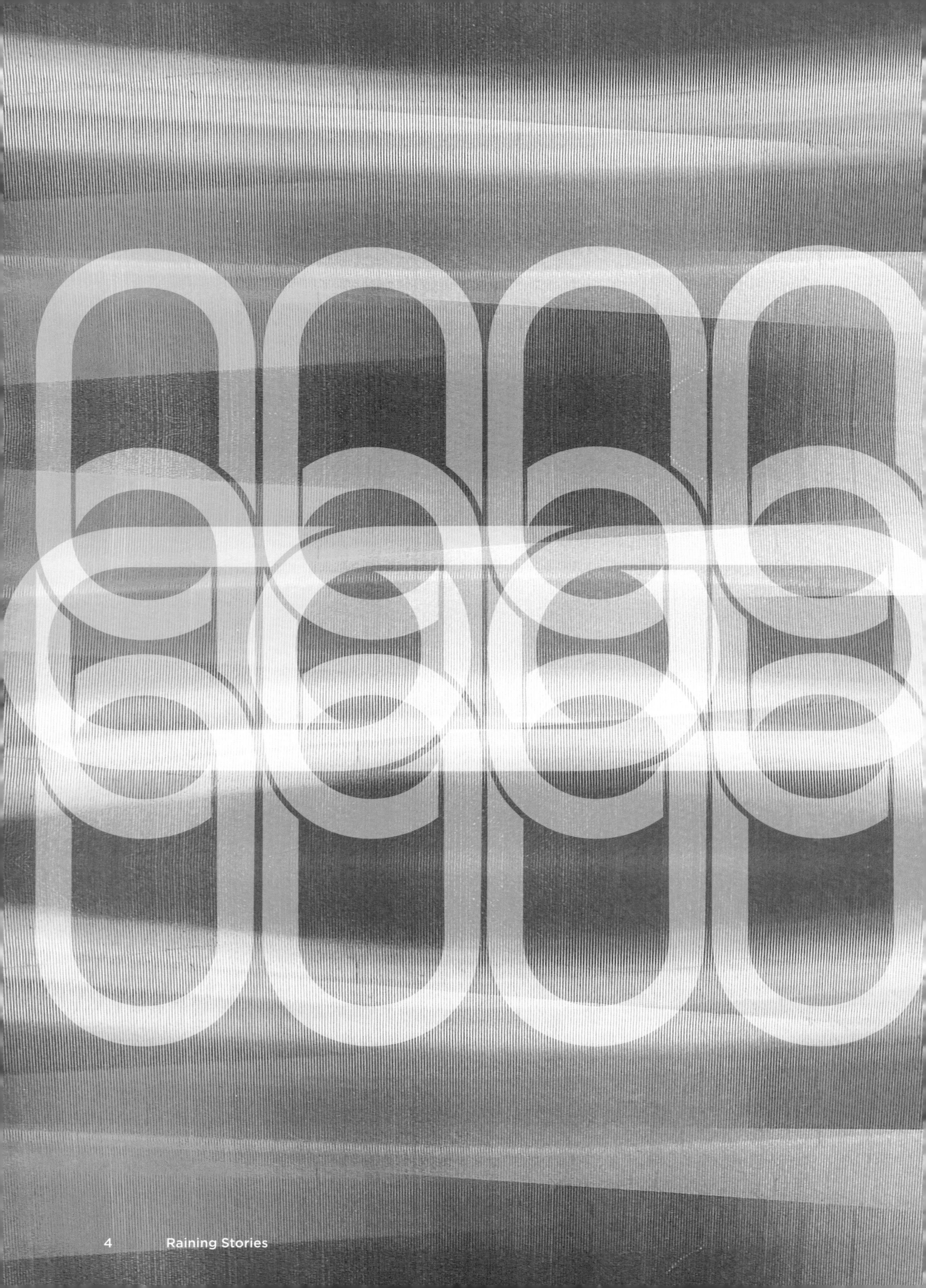

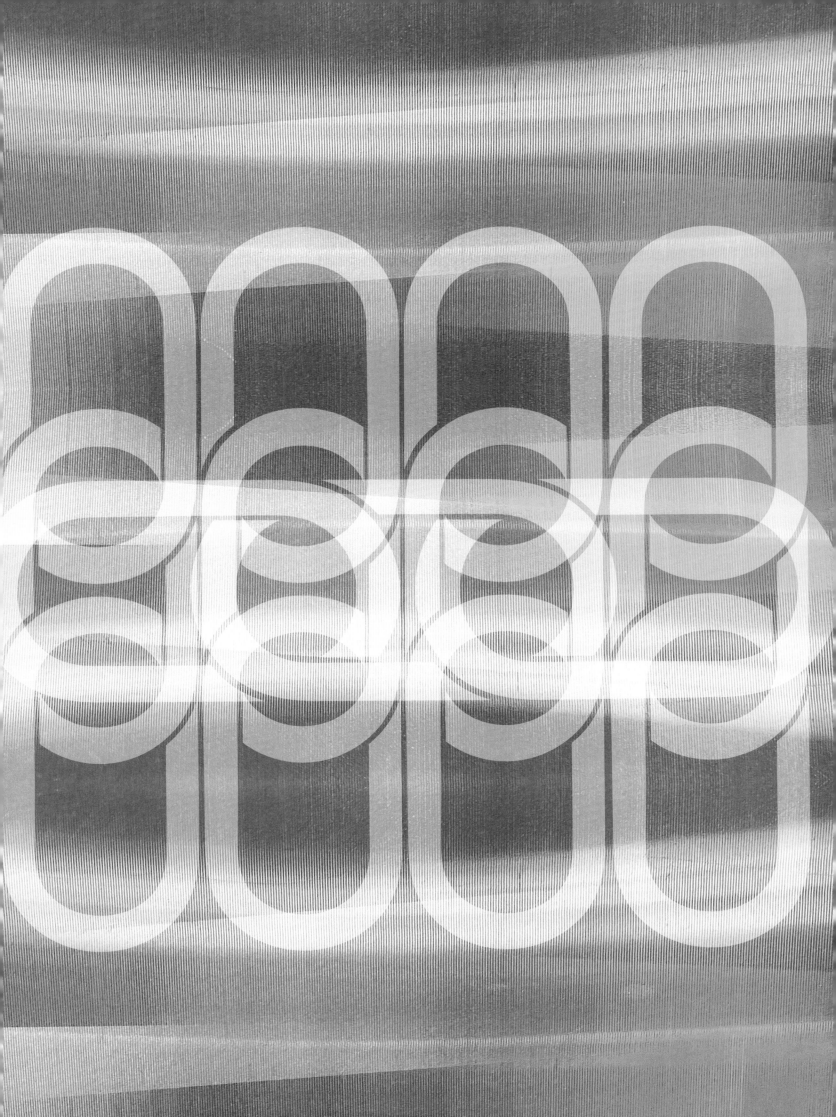

NETHERLANDS
PAVILION
EXPO
2020
DUBAI

RAINING STORIES

Netherlands Pavilion Expo 2020 Dubai

nai010 publishers

FORE-WORD

Tom de Bruijn

Uniting Water, Energy & Food

To feed, house and secure the almost 10 billion people that will inhabit the world by 2050, we have to rethink the way we use scarce resources and meet the growing demand for water, energy and food as efficiently and sustainably as possible.

During Expo 2020 Dubai the Netherlands is showcasing technologies and innovations at the nexus of water, energy and food – the aim is to show how working together can help achieve the Sustainable Development Goals.

The Netherlands Pavilion is all about making smart and sustainable connections between these resources, as a way to create innovative solutions for global issues like water scarcity, the energy transition and food security. By using water and energy more sustainably, we can increase food production and enhance our resilience in the face of climate change.

Designed as a recyclable miniature world with a naturally controlled climate, the pavilion shows how a combination of unique innovations makes it possible to extract water from air, harvest food and generate electricity. In Dubai's dry desert climate, the Netherlands has created a temporary biotope. Its unique design allows visitors to experience the circular connection between water, energy and food in an engaging way, while keeping the pavilion's ecological footprint as small as possible.

Just as there can be no food without water and energy, innovations wouldn't exist without international collaboration between governments, businesses and knowledge institutions that connect people, their minds, their expertise and their skills.

The open, inclusive and inventive approach taken by Dutch businesses and knowledge institutions allows them to work with partners in the Gulf region to promote more efficient water use, facilitate the transition to renewable energy, and enhance food security.

At our pavilion, we're reaching out to the Gulf and the rest of the world, providing a platform where people can come together, learn from each other, discuss solutions to unite water, energy and food, and inspire each other to think creatively and – most importantly – holistically.

Complementing your visit to our pavilion, this book is a wonderful guide to our history and ground-breaking sustainable innovations – a 'take-home pavilion' if you like. After 31 March 2022, the pavilion will be gone forever, leaving no footprint behind. This valuable reference book will preserve our legacy.

Welcome to the Netherlands Pavilion!

Tom de Bruijn
Minister for Foreign Trade and Development Cooperation

CONTENTS

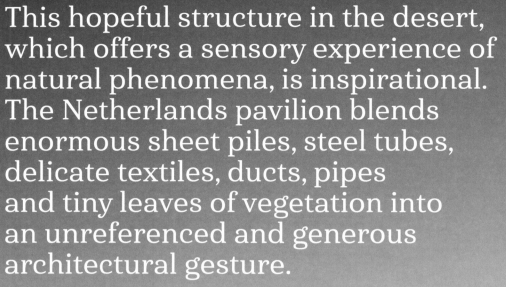

This hopeful structure in the desert, which offers a sensory experience of natural phenomena, is inspirational. The Netherlands pavilion blends enormous sheet piles, steel tubes, delicate textiles, ducts, pipes and tiny leaves of vegetation into an unreferenced and generous architectural gesture.

The Netherlands

RAINING STORIES

Jaap Huisman

We humans want to go up, we climb the stairs, the slopes and the mountains and we do all that to catch the light. For centuries it has been like this, imagined and expressed in landscapes and buildings: the Acropolis, the Borobudur, Mont Ventoux and Mexico's Mayan temples, they all rise up from the flat land. Up we must go, because it appears to come natural to us, like the lemmings' migration to the sea. Up equals progress, divine inspiration and optimism.

Down. This appears to be an unnatural movement. After all, in Greek mythology the journey down is the dreaded descent into the underworld, where a ferryman rows you across to an unknown and dark shore. A place where, as a human, you do not want to be – until you are freed. By a singer with a harp perhaps. The underworld is the unknown, mysterious and perhaps threatening all at once, which is why we shun the descent.

The fact that this is changing is partly due to climate change; the increasing heat is making an increasing number of places on earth uninhabitable. Conditions of life are under duress; the desert is closing in on us.

STRATEGICAL

Sun and darkness, drought and moisture: they are the opposites of the Netherlands pavilion at Expo 2020 Dubai. Geographically interesting, because the Emirates are a link between East and West, North and South. This is the first time that one of the Gulf states is hosting a global exhibition. Can it get any more strategic? It's a challenge for the Netherlands to present itself here: Dubai alone accommodates more than 200 businesses. In 2018, the Netherlands exported 14 billion euros worth of goods and knowledge to the Gulf region and imported goods and knowledge worth 7.7 billion. Although economically and commercially the World Expo is a key player in international relations, geologically the chosen spot could hardly be more challenging. Temperatures rising up to 45 degrees in summer, a plain filled with grains of sand from which it's impossible to build even a sandcastle – the structure of desert sand is quite different from that of beach sand.

What is the Netherlands doing there? The land of dikes and polders, waterways and canals, mud and clay? A larger contrast is hardly imaginable. Sun versus rain, for another thing. Barrenness versus fertility. But let a thousand flowers bloom and who knows, maybe one will take root, even in Dubai.

ARTIFICIALITY

However opposite they are, there is one important similarity between Dubai and the Netherlands and that is the artificiality of their landscapes and buildings. Just like the Netherlands has reinvented its landscape over and over again by pumping out water through pumping stations and windmills and by building dikes, so Dubai is trying to create life in the desert. It sprays islands in the shape of palm leaves in the sea, it has indoor ski slopes and ice rinks, it has shopping malls in which the air conditioning blows you away, it has sprays that cool the pedestrians in the streets. In short, its urban designers are doing everything they can to mitigate the climate and ensure and increase liveability. Just like we in the Netherlands try to keep our heads above water, for example on terps in retention areas.

Reinventing the landscape

From a forecourt, we descend into the underworld. We want to, because as we descend it gets cooler, while aboveground the sun has been beating down on us mercilessly. We smell something, feel something, in the limbo of this descent. Sounds impose themselves, the swishing of wind turbine blades, the mooing of cows. We've been given umbrellas – what, umbrellas in the desert?! What is that smell? Plants, perhaps fungi. We also smell something typically Dutch. It's the smell of the oldest polder in the Netherlands, Mastenbroek, which artist Birthe Leemeijer has captured in a perfume that runs through glass pipes along the walls. They drip in places, allowing us to sprinkle our hands and feet with it. Ah, so this is how the Netherlands smell, like wet grass. For desert dwellers, smelling it must be an unprecedented experience.

We descend to get cooler, while aboveground the sun has been beating down on us mercilessly.

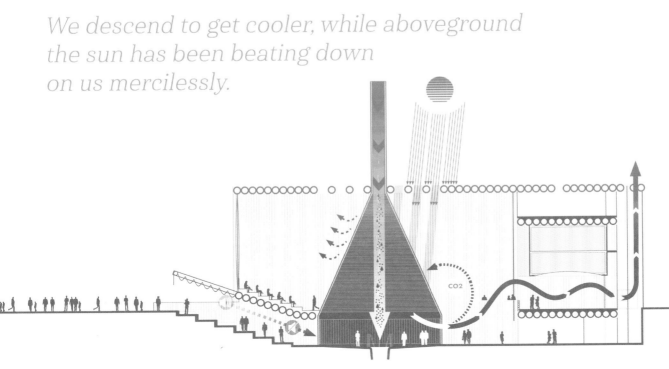

The surroundings give us no clues. The downward track is sheltered by sheet piling that has already begun to rust. Due to the Covid-19 outbreak, it has been here since 2020. No problem, it will be dismantled and sent back to the supplier somewhere in 2022. For like all of Dubai's buildings, this building – if it is a building – is temporary, borrowed, provisional. No, of course this does not apply to Dubai's skyscrapers, although it is conceivable that in a few centuries' time, even they will have been buried under desert sand or crushed by a storm. Not so the Netherlands pavilion, which will simply disappear, dissolve in the desert, not even leaving a hole in the ground. Nothing is forever. This building thus breaks with the laws of architecture, which assume that what is built is as indestructible as a Greek Temple.

This building breaks with the laws of architecture

BIOTOPE

So rather than with a project or product, Michiel Raaphorst and Rudolph Eilander of architecture office V8 Architects won the tender with a concept. To be more precise: the pavilion is a biotope in which natural conditions are imitated. If the Netherlands is a human-made country, then its Word Expo pavilion is a display of knowledge and innovation. The pavilion is a miniature world in which everything is connected to everything else. We've been exporting tulips, seeds, water systems and yes, even architecture and infrastructure for a long time, but times have changed. Knowhow, and the transfer of knowledge in the fields of agriculture, water management and climate control, have replaced them. Abstractions have supplanted concrete products and this resonates in the shape of the pavilion. The theme of the pavilion is the story, in fact it is raining stories inside. Using a bit of imagination you could call the structure a fata morgana – they frequently occur in the desert – in this case, a fata morgana of a future reality.

The question of how to make a polder blossom is equivalent to the question of how to make a desert fertile in one of the most arid places in the world. The answer lies at a depth of five metres, in the soil that is accessed by a ramp. Yes, please put up your umbrella once you have reached the underworld. At its deepest point, we encounter a mountain of food created by Dutch horticulture at its best. On the mountains tomatoes are ripening, rosemary and thyme are coming to

A mountain of food

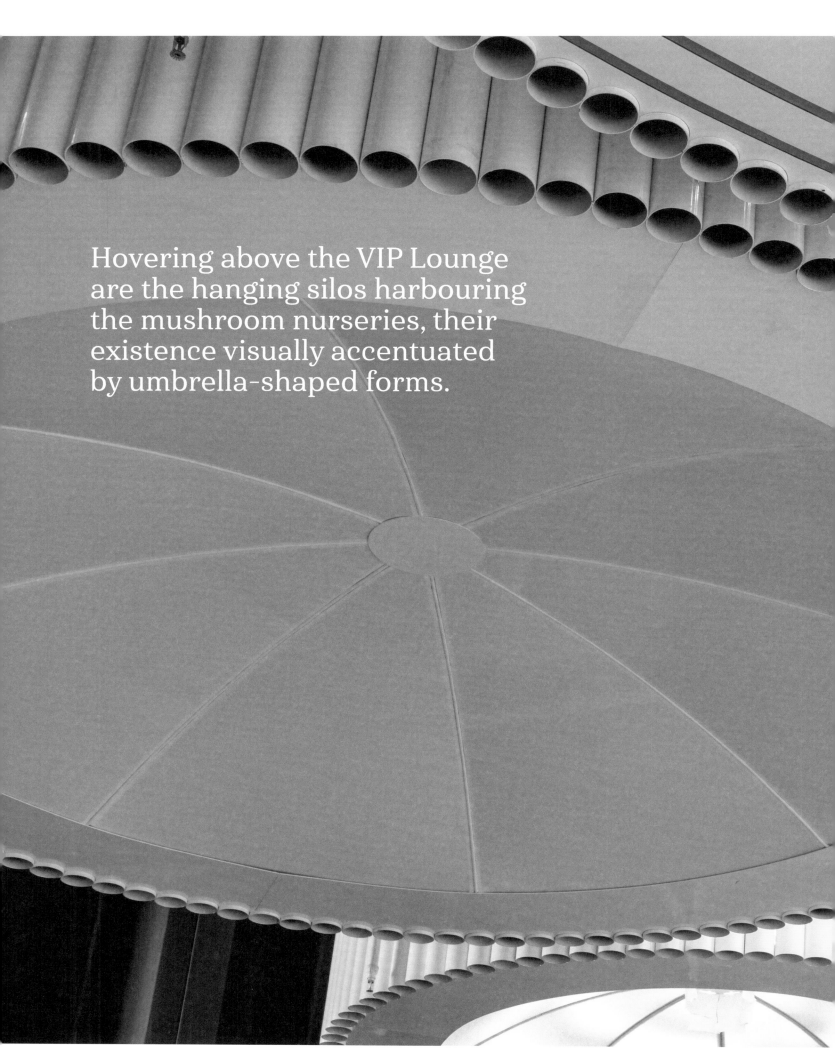

Hovering above the VIP Lounge are the hanging silos harbouring the mushroom nurseries, their existence visually accentuated by umbrella-shaped forms.

life, asparagus are taking root, even. And then there are the walls of this space. They are covered and clad with oyster mushrooms. Aha, that was the slightly fungal smell we noticed before. Down here, all of our senses are addressed.

No, those are not angels or stewards in slick suits or outfits guiding or surrounding the experience, that would distort the message or rather the story. They're wearing denim overalls, they're basic and therefore not divine. They're the messengers of a future that centres on the liveability of the planet, that is, on food in conjunction with energy and water. Water? Is that the gurgling of a waterfall we hear? Is that drops we feel?

AMBITIONS AND ACHIEVEMENTS

Most World Expos cast their shadow ahead. We climbed the stairs, we went all the way to the top of the Eiffel Tower and afterwards, we returned to earth: that is how it has been for a century and a half. When all is said and done, Word Expos showcase national achievements and ambitions and leave a trail of new technology behind. In fact, it's extremely rare for a building to remain standing to become the icon of a city like

World Expos leave a trail of new technology behind

the Eiffel Tower in Paris, the Atomium in Brussels and the Crystal Palace in London. More and more often they become the beacon of a new district or area, for example in Seville, Shanghai and also Hannover. Dubai is no exception. Besides a number of central buildings that are being given a public function, a new residential district is taking possession of this piece of desert. All that remains is the documentation of the concepts, the ideas and inventions that belong to the spirit of the time. Few of the national pavilions will remain standing. The plots will be renovated to create a future, diverse residential district.

The iconic architecture the Netherlands and other countries have presented at previous Word Expos appears and is a thing of a distant past. Have we now come round to 'please, just act normally'? No, that's not it. Although the architects of V8 trained in Delft to design beautiful buildings and put this into practice at Erick van Egeraat's office, they discovered that architecture is more than four walls, a ceiling and a foundation. V8's Michiel Raaphorst about winning the tender: 'We came up with the theme of water, energy and food through teamwork. We started thinking about ways to give substance to circularity. This starting point appealed

Normally, a chimney is meant
to discharge smoke, but here
its emissions contribute to
air and moisture circulation.
The pavilion is therefore a kind
of factory, an engine room.

to the Ministry of Foreign Affairs and the Netherlands Enterprise Agency (RVO). Use of local materials, thinking about repurposing, back to the bare necessities. It was like traveling to Mars in Dubai.'

ART AND TECHNOLOGY

This meant the collaboration between artists and technicians, researchers and engineers was crucial. To realize its plan V8 Architects called in Swiss construction company ExpoMobilia. ExpoMobilia is an experienced construction company; the business specializes in temporary and semipermanent buildings that rely heavily on cost calculation, logistics and of course dismantling when the party is over. They know the ropes, having previously worked on pavilions at the World Expo's of Astana (2017) and Milan (2015). According to the Swiss, the climatological conditions were particularly demanding, especially because they were building a pavilion in the hot summer months. Unlike the World Cup in Qatar, where poor working conditions were at issue, Dubai could not afford any faux pas. In fact, the participating countries drew up a strict protocol with which ExpoMobilia had to comply as well.

Collaboration between artists and technicians, researchers and engineers

In the end the realization of the pavilion became a collective process. It involved a great deal of consultation and coordination. Witteveen+Bos drew for and on the construction, even though it does not play a major part in this 'building pit'. The integrated story is the guiding principle. In all likelihood the most important message the pavilion sends is about the ability of artists to come up with solutions to global problems.

Or at least, that's the connecting link that curator Monique Ruhe searched for and found while she was selecting the art. After all, the problems we face are substantial and urgent: climate change, drought and flooding, not to mention the food shortages that threaten large parts of the world. This is why Ruhe also chose a giant, sturdy clock by Joep van Lieshout that warns us that it is now five minutes to twelve; Van Lieshout also contributed an hourglass. Time is ticking; waiting or running away are no longer options. This is also demonstrated by the photographs by Kadir van Lohuizen, who first captured the consequences of climate change and now the food production in the Netherlands.

So no iconic architecture. 'It's not about beauty,' says one of the partners. In the year 2021, impressiveness is no longer an issue. The new buzzwords are sensible and

Sensible and sustainable

sustainable, with sustainable being used as a container term for recyclable, biodegradable, leaving no footprint. In other words: leave the desert in peace when the party is over. The Netherlands pavilion is not in the sustainability district without reason.

INVENTIONS

Perhaps we should call it non-architecture, this cube in Dubai, which looks like a factory or a shed. An engine room, says Ruhe, meant to make people aware of their surroundings. In this room, the descent and the adventures we have underway are the most important. Suddenly, images of the Dutch production landscape flash by inside the umbrellas, on screens or in pictures. On the official National Day opening Berndnaut Smilde conjures up a cloud of which photographs are taken that remain as mementos. Theo Janssen moves his beach animals about the auditorium and then there's Vilma Henkelman, a ceramicist whose vases and urns breathe the spirit of the desert; their rust-coloured hue makes them look like modern archaeological finds.

In terms of art, the pavilion is where the action will be for six months, but the track cannot be too long, because visitors' attention span is short, as exhibition maker Mark de Jong (Kossmanndejong) knows. Clichés like windmills, clogs and tulips are out of the question. If you want to present yourself as an agrarian world power, rather than just windmills you'll have to show some windmills – or rather, wind turbines – as well as greenhouses and new inventions such as lab meat. And of course the war that the Netherlands wages on the water. This has become a major export item. If there's a flood somewhere, or some metropolis has gotten its feet wet, the Dutch engineers turn out.

Agrarian world power

Down and down the ramp descends into the pavilion. The corridors are relatively dark and narrow but not too narrow, because experience shows that the curious will visit the Expo in droves, and at a time when people have to keep their distance due to Covid-19, congestion is the thing to avoid.

PANTHEON

We opted for a ramp, says Mark de Jong, because the alternative – a big lift – would result in too many visitors in a small space. A ramp also allows wheelchair users to get to know the subterranean Netherlands.

As we descend further down we suddenly face a sliding door. This only opens when there is room for a fresh group of people. This area is supposed to make visitors go oh! and ah! because of the huge cone V8 Architects designed, a dome that runs into a chimney on the roof. The chimney does not process smoke, but allows the air to circulate, which is necessary to make and keep conditions in the interior pleasant. Air is drawn in, cooled by an installation and distributed through the space. Because it is not only outside that a scorching heat reigns, people bring their own body heat into the interior as well.

It's a theatrical space, an underground Pantheon in which, at the very top, daylight is screened off by a stained-glass window by Marjan van Aubel. It's not a window in the classic sense, but rather an ingenious construction of wafer-thin solar panels.

Visitor experience: from the queueing area through the control room into the cone.

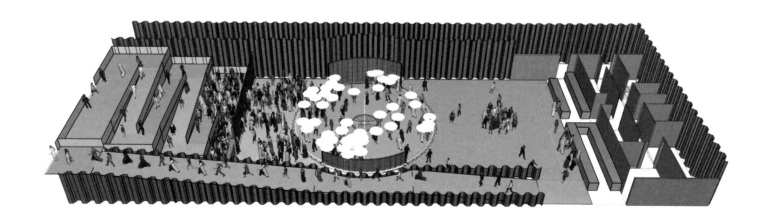

Thanks to photosynthesis these solar panels are the energy source that feeds the pavilion. Without those panels, the ingenious cooling system on the basis of water currents would not work. Van Aubel has succeeded – finally someone has! – in giving solar panels an acceptable appearance, ensuring we would rather have hers in our fields than the existing production panels. Again, it is an artist who closes the gap between design and innovation.

And this touches on the core of the Netherlands pavilion: everything is connected to everything else. Each ingredient has a function. Take the curtain that Amsterdam-based Buro Belén had woven to screen off the VIP area.
It shows that textile innovation can also produce aesthetically pleasing and tactile results. You want to touch it and feel it, and it also dampens sound.

This pavilion is all about interplay and the sum of the parts. Unlike previous World Expo editions, innovation trumps the aesthetics of architecture. Inside, in the relative darkness, is where the story is told.

Whether the character of this pavilion is following or leading is hard to say.
V8 Architects has put a ball in the field that artists, designers and engineers have then

kicked around. The keyword is circularity. This means that the pavilion transcends the container term 'sustainability'. Sustainability is not even an issue, because by the end of March 2022 the final verdict will be: demolition. Circularity means that everything that human beings produce on the earth's surface goes back to the source, either by reuse or by transience. Food is processed or consumed; the sheet piles are broken down. Some parts will be reused.

WATER AS A SOURCE OF LIFE

The experience continues. Inside the cone, visitors are asked to unfold their umbrellas as a steady rain is falling; the water is collected in a well. Like everywhere else on earth, water is pivotal: it generates life, it refreshes and cools us, it's the conditio sine qua non for food production and consumption. Where would we be without water or, beneath this dome, humidity? This is the contribution of engineering office Witteveen+Bos, which designed a climate installation powered by tap water. The office made every effort to avoid energy-guzzling air conditioning. Air conditioning is only indispensable in the small outbuildings behind the pavilion, because a restaurant, kiosk and toilet depend on it.

How do you make rain in the desert?
That's one of the many innovative questions answered by this pavilion. When V8 Architects and the consortium won the tender, they selected sculptor Ap Verheggen as a prominent participant. He is the link between the three elements. For years, Verheggen has been working on a machine with a nozzle that can convert moisture in the air into rain. Condensation is the source of life, the motor of our survival. For it's really not all that dry in Dubai. Images show how the skyscrapers are sometimes wrapped in ribbons of mist, leaving panoramas less than clear. And anyone who has ever spent a night in the desert knows that in the morning dew will hover over the grains of sand. Verheggen has made these almost unthinkable phenomena concrete. He was right to apply for a patent for this invention, after all, his find deserves to be called downright revolutionary and it's a find without which this biotope could not have existed.

How do you make rain
in the desert?

The sprinkler system with heads by artist Ap Verheggen is the main link between all of the ingredients in the pavilion: without its 'droplets', the food mountain cannot grow and the climate would remain too dry.

Inside the cone,
the damp climate
stimulates the
growth of edible
mushrooms.

It's raining stories inside the pavilion. They're not too heavy, too pedantic or too educational. They're casual, rather. Before we reach the cone we see figures representing water, energy and food. Those are the three themes commissioner RVO had issued the participating consortia. This Word Expo addresses other subjects as well, including mobility and technology, fields in which famous architects manifest themselves, the usual suspects from the star class, like Santiago Calatrava and Norman Foster. Compared to this, the Dutch presentation is a model of modesty and restraint. The message has to do the job.

CIRCULARITY

Creating a circularity machine, that was the starting point from which V8 Architects set to work. What they wanted to achieve was a sensory experience. Everything that emerges at the building site will disappear again or be demolished. As if a meteorite had crashed on the outskirts of Dubai, that's the temporal feeling evoked, a hole that leaves no trace. It's remarkable and perhaps even historic that the Netherlands manifests itself with a structure that exists and eliminates its existence at the same time. That's also different than at previous Word Expos.

Sensory experience

Anyone traveling to Hannover – the site of the 2000 edition – today will find a pavilion of which the concrete is slowly crumbling and rotting away whereas at the time of its completion, it was a display of innovation with trees on the roof, a nursery on a lower floor and a water curtain for a façade. By the way, the architects of this tower, MVRDV, are going to breathe new life into it and give it a new use.

Witteveen+Bos's Steven Delfgaauw recalls that at the first meeting with V8 Architects, they discussed whether using 3D-printed exterior walls was an option. That certainly would have been a major innovation! However, printing concrete would have been at odds with the pursuit of circularity, because the pavilion was not supposed to outlive a maximum of six months. Dismantling concrete would not have been in line with the plan and it would also have used up too much space. Plots at the Word Expo are not all that spacious. A small gate accesses the interior, which makes sheet piles a good alternative. The fact that they are corroding away already is really all right, because in the end they'll go to a demolition firm or old iron shop anyway. The pavilion is in fact as sober a the Dutch landscape, as short-lived as a winter with natural ice: once it starts to melt, the fun is over.

NEXUS

The logo KesselsKramer designed for the Netherlands pavilion is significant. It's a link of three ellipses, in red, white and blue of course, which together form a chain and stand for the themes of water, food and energy. It's the stepping stone for the stories that are told, in fact a nexus (knot) between pragmatism and poetry. Pragmatic, if not urgent, is the question of how to feed the world population in the coming decades; poetic is the way in which water seeps into our existence, as an abstract flow of life.

Local materials

In Dubai, however, the story focuses on reuse and the limits that can be pushed. It was therefore natural for the architects to use local materials, not in the least because bringing building materials in from the Netherlands would conflict with the circularity principle. Although these elements are not visible in the pavilion, this is exactly the point – more than ever before, this is a presentation that comprises the backgrounds and reasons that come with climate-neutral and biobased building in this day and age, rather than visible elements.

This is a pavilion that calls for innovative art, as Ruhe told the commissioner, Foreign Affairs. The story of a solution has to be told. Free and independent art happen to fit the pavilion design very well and also demonstrate the creativity that is available in the Netherlands.

LIVEABILITY

Folding our umbrellas we leave the cone, the underground Pantheon. Our senses have been stimulated, the sensation of a future experience has taken hold of our memories. So what was the story we were told? Was it the story of humankind trying to survive in all kinds of circumstances, of how we're always looking for a way out, towards supreme liveability? Of how we can also find a source in an unreachable place beneath desert sand and rocks? Of how we, despite abundant rainfall, can wade through the streets and wait for the sun to come out? Actually, the architecture of V8 Architects, Witteveen+Bos and ExpoMobilia is a lesson in humility. We make buildings because they shelter us from the sun or the rain – in that sense it makes no difference whether the pavilion is in Dubai or in, say, the water-rich Dutch province of Zeeland. But the fact that this building can function like a machine adds another dimension. It provides water, food and energy.

Perhaps that is all we, as human beings, need. On 31 March 2022 we will fold our umbrellas for good, all of the asparagus shoots, oyster mushrooms and other edibles will have been harvested and it will stop raining. That's not to say Dubai will remain dry afterwards. But the construction pit will close. We didn't have to go up to find the source of life, but down.

Dust to Dust.

The pavilion functions like a machine

DUST TO DUST.

Consortium
Statements

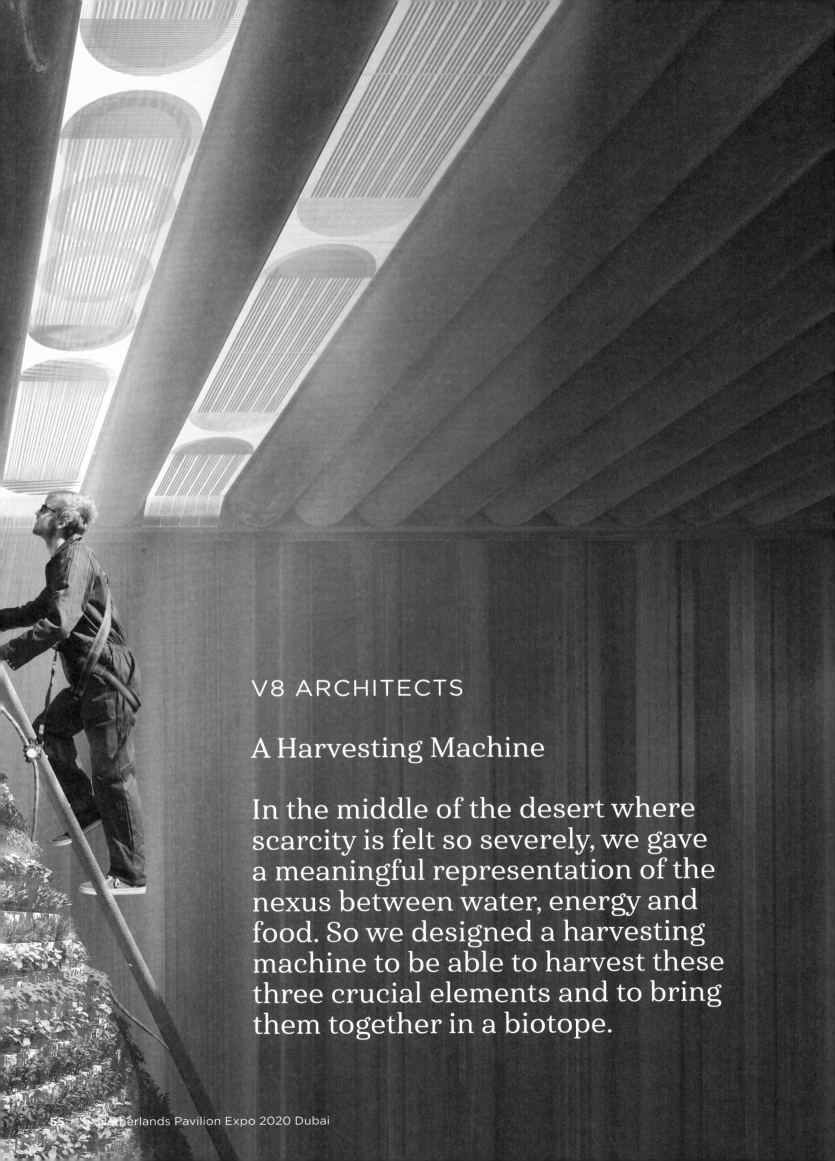

V8 ARCHITECTS

A Harvesting Machine

In the middle of the desert where scarcity is felt so severely, we gave a meaningful representation of the nexus between water, energy and food. So we designed a harvesting machine to be able to harvest these three crucial elements and to bring them together in a biotope.

EXPOMOBILIA

The Netherlands pavilion at Dubai Expo 2020 is a unique build for Expomobilia, master crafstmen of temporary structures. Materials used were sourced locally and are reusable, recyclable or biodegradable.

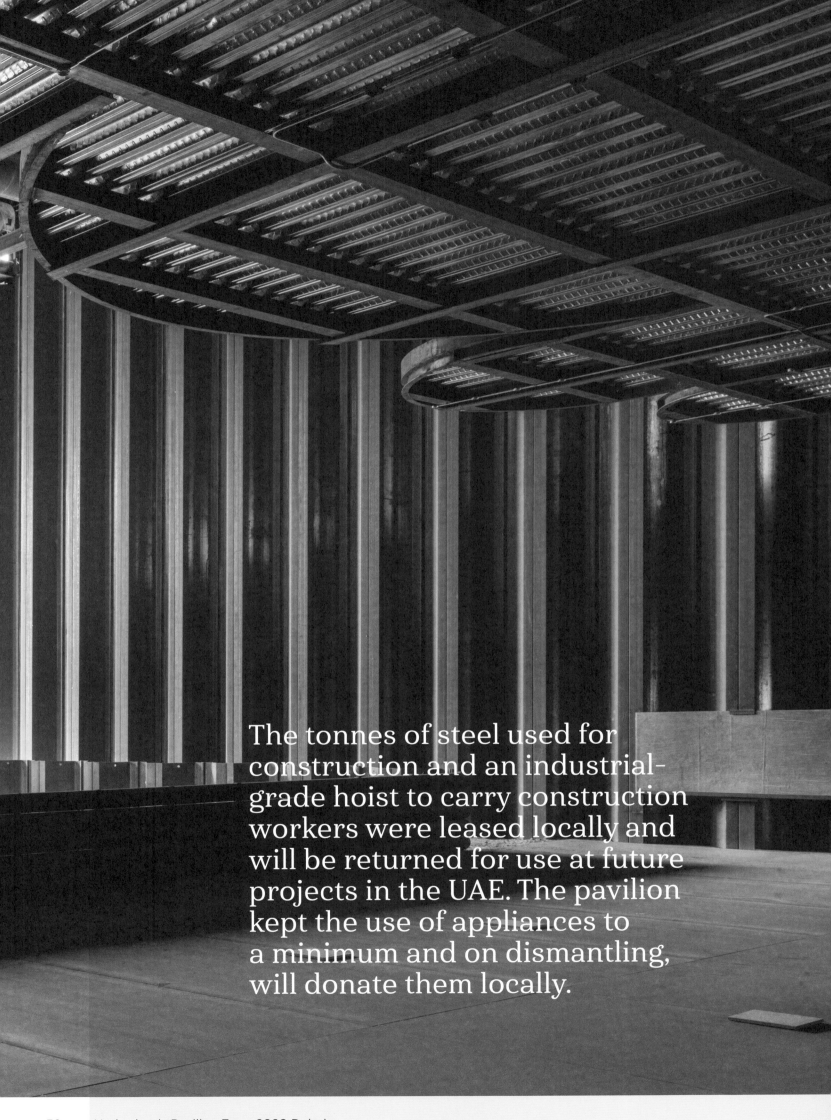

The tonnes of steel used for construction and an industrial-grade hoist to carry construction workers were leased locally and will be returned for use at future projects in the UAE. The pavilion kept the use of appliances to a minimum and on dismantling, will donate them locally.

KOSSMANNDEJONG

A Meaningful Statement

The visitor experience of the Netherlands Pavilion is designed as a multisensory journey that demonstrates to the visitor that it requires an integral approach to food production, energy generation and freshwater management to solve global problems.

The pavilion provides a unique multisensory experience by incorporating sounds, projections, lighting, smells and things that can be touched and tasted. These experiences also guide visitors through the pavilion in an intuitive, non-verbal way.

The powerful idea of harvesting water from desert air and letting it rain down inside the pavilion inspired the use of umbrellas to visualize the motto of the pavilion: raining stories.

The pavilion is a machine, a factory. But also a performance in which the front of house staff plays an important role. Dressed in clothes made of recycled denim, inspired by workers' overalls, they bring the factory to life.

The corporate uniforms for the Netherlands Pavilion are 100 per cent circular, consisting of 50 per cent recycled textile and 50 per cent recycled polyester. The clothing will be returned after the Expo so it can be recycled into new corporate clothing. This means a saving of 99 per cent of the water, 40 per cent of the CO_2 emissions and 40 per cent of the energy necessary to make these clothes.

WITTEVEEN+BOS

In terms of construction, the 'Building Pit' is not the main issue; the story and the accompanying innovation are the main players in this case. To give substance to the concept of circularity, we proposed using sheet piling that can be given a second life instead of 3-D printed concrete material.

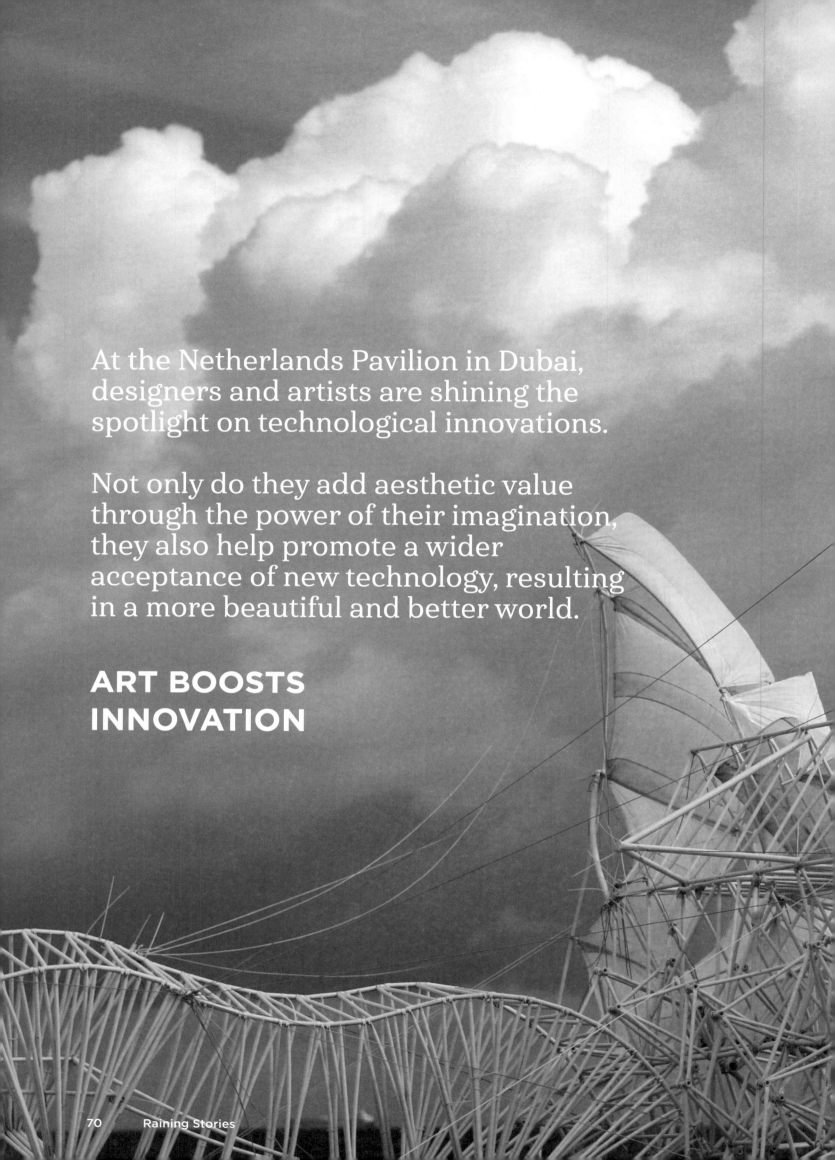

At the Netherlands Pavilion in Dubai, designers and artists are shining the spotlight on technological innovations.

Not only do they add aesthetic value through the power of their imagination, they also help promote a wider acceptance of new technology, resulting in a more beautiful and better world.

ART BOOSTS INNOVATION

Tracy Metz

MAKE RAIN WHILE THE SUN SHINES

Tracy Metz is a journalist, author and speaker based in Amsterdam. She was a member of the Dutch Delta Commission that advised government on water safety for the coming one to two centuries. She wrote a book about the changing approach in Dutch water management called 'Sweet&Salt: Water and the Dutch', published by nai010 publishers.

'If we make smart use of technology,' says Michiel Raaphorst of V8 Architects, 'we can help nature move in the right direction. In the post-industrial age, nature and human ingenuity can go hand in hand. That is what the contribution of this and future generations to this planet should be.'

Tracy Metz

The first time I visited Dubai, I saw many things I expected – huge polished shopping centres, camel races, men in sparkling white dishdashas and women in flowing abayas beset with Swarovski stones – but I was also in for a big surprise. All over the city I saw billboards advertising 'Green Development'. Green as in ecological, I assumed? Actually, no. These developments were fancy residential complexes with lawns and even golf courses. Green, yes, but not as I had imagined.

It takes a lot of effort and energy to desalinate enough sea water to keep these lawns and golf courses green in the desert. So what are the alternatives? The pavilion of the Netherlands at Expo 2020 Dubai is dedicated to what its designers, architecture firm V8, call 'the Nexus': the intimate connection between water, energy and food. Normally it rains no more than 25 days out of the year in Dubai – but the Dutch design team can make it rain every day of the World Expo – well, inside the pavilion. (Umbrellas are provided.)

Dubai itself has of course already been casting around for alternatives, given that the United Arab Emirates is one of the world's most water-scarce nations. Since 2017 it is home to the largest 'water farm' of the American company Source, which is active in 48 countries on five continents. Source uses so-called hydropanels to create fresh, clean drinking water from sunlight and air, 1,5 million litres per year for Dubai alone.

WAR ON WATER

Before we delve into how it works, let's first take a look at the centuries-old relationship of the Netherlands to water. The landscape and the climate could not be more different from Dubai's desert. A good third of the country is below sea level, incidentally the third where 70 per cent of the GDP is generated. It is only kept habitable by the dunes that keep the

sea in the west at bay and the dikes that keep back the rivers flowing in from the European hinterland to the east.

For centuries, the Dutch felt that they were at war with water, and they manipulated the natural system at will, pumping water out to reclaim arable land, raising or lowering the groundwater table to accommodate cows and agricultural machinery, narrowing the rivers to make shipping more efficient. The mentality was utilitarian and dominating: water was at the service of man.

Now, however, that is changing. Not only under pressure of climate change, but also as the consequences of the long-term disruption of the hydrological system have become ever more apparent. It takes a while, but the approach is moving towards 'building with nature': making more room for water in combination with a more flexible system of defences. Who would have thought that in some places the dikes would not be raised, but actually lowered to allow controlled flooding?

There are other changes afoot, too. The Netherlands always needed to pump excess water out to sea, but now with sea level rise and hotter, drier summers, it is facing the possibility that it might run short of fresh water for agriculture, industry and human consumption. And in July of 2021, just a couple months before the opening of the World Expo, Germany, Belgium and the Netherlands were taken by surprise when heavy rainfall caused floods – in the middle of the summer, the dry season! – that took over 200 lives in Germany and Belgium and caused hundreds of millions of euros worth of damage. It was a dramatic wakeup call to revise flood defences and early warning systems. Will the rest of the world still say 'Bring in the Dutch!' to help rethink and redesign their climate strategy?

'The Nexus': the intimate connection between water, energy and food.

CIRCULAR CLIMATE SYSTEM

The world is facing water crises of various kinds, which come down to: too much (floods), too little (fires and drought) and too dirty (unsafe for consumption). And the world looks to events like the World Expo for innovative ideas – like those behind the Netherlands pavilion.

Natural phenomena such as condensation, solar energy, photosynthesis, humidity and temperature transmission are brought together to create a miniature, autonomous, circular climate system that provides water, energy and food. Dutch artist Ap Verheggen has devised a system that – if all goes according to plan – will produce 800 litres of clean water a day, in the form of condensation.

Inside the cone, the water will be used to irrigate mushrooms, which are themselves a source of food. The mushrooms moreover produce carbon dioxide, which in the natural process of photosynthesis is transformed in combination with sunlight into oxygen and carbohydrates that nourish plants. This is the Nexus, a circular system powered simply by the energy of the sun, a resource generously available in Dubai.

And it must be. In order to keep our planet habitable, we will have to find solutions that go beyond those that engineers and technicians have invented so far. In Dubai, the Dutch may have found a new way of building with nature and living with water.

Ap Verheggen

ART BOOSTS INNOVATION

'We have to test the limits of existing technology to make it adapt to the changing conditions of our planet.'

Ap Verheggen is a sculptor with a technological streak and a strong sense of urgency about climate change. His SunGlacier is a potential gamechanger when it comes to securing safe drinking water.

Not oil, not coal, not minerals like coltan and tantalum, but plain old water will be the most coveted natural resource in the near future. Climate change is accelerating desertification in tropical and subtropical countries, making them practically uninhabitable. Other regions are flooded by excess water from melting snow and ice combined with increasingly torrential rains that endanger the supply of potable water. The availability of safe drinking water is already a major issue in many parts of the world, with some 750 million people lacking access to it.

The situation is only going to get worse. Ap Verheggen found out how urgent the situation truly is in 2009 when he installed sculptures with GPS trackers on glaciers in Greenland. The trackers enabled him to monitor the ice melting and the ice floes' 'migration' towards the ocean. Alarmingly, the trackers were gone within a matter of months.

Verheggen doesn't just use his brand of technology-infused art to create awareness about impending ecological disasters, he also works on solutions. His biggest claim to fame is the SunGlacier, a machine that harvests water from air. It is batteryless, has no moving parts and is powered by solar panels. The magic is worked by a Peltier cooler, a thermoelectric heat pump normally used in the computer industry to cool chips to well below ambient temperatures. In the SunGlacier it turns vaporized water molecules into condensation.

Verheggen worked on the SunGlacier for over seven years. Its development received a boost when the Dutch Ministry of Defence invited the artist/inventor to test his machine in the Malian desert. It proved successful in temperatures just shy of 50ºC, but Verheggen felt there was room for improvement and designed over 50 new prototypes. The result of this finetuning will be presented at the World Expo in Dubai. A 20-foot container atop the Netherlands pavilion will provide hundreds of litres of water a day in a region where water usually has to be extracted from deep wells or imported by tanker.

That the humidity in the desert is still high is proven by the mist that hides the skyscrapers from view halfway down.

Dubai has a high relative humidity, the average highest humidity is between 82 and 92 per cent, the lowest values are between 25 and 45 per cent. The highest humidity is measured in the winter, in May it is at its lowest point.

Berndnaut Smilde

ART BOOSTS INNOVATION

'I see clouds as temporary sculptures made out of almost nothing.'

Berndnaut Smilde has mastered the art of cloud making – indoor cloud making. His meteorological manipulations force us to take a better look at the environment and consider what's real.

His clouds were one of Time magazine's 10 Best Inventions of 2012, super collector Charles Saatchi immediately bought one photo for his private museum, and once it was posted online, the footage went viral in no time. Nimbus II's appeal is immediate yet illusive, making it an instant success. Berndnaut Smilde's work of art is recognizable as a cloud, yet it is somehow floating indoors – obviously not its usual habitat. It's a natural phenomenon, but man-made. The image infuses something as mundane as the promise of rain with poetic surrealism.

It took Smilde years to perfect his cloud-making technique. It still requires elaborate preparations and exactly the right conditions for his magic to work. A combination of a fog machine, high humidity, a low temperature and the right lighting causes moisture droplets to cling to smoke and form a cloud.

Smilde has since created nimbuses around the globe. He even whipped one up in the bone-dry Pilbara region of Western Australia, which looked just as out of place as the one in a sixteenth-century chapel.

After coalescing, Smilde's clouds last just a few moments. They live on in the pictures he takes of them, which are, in his opinion, the real works of art. This adds to the mystery of this domesticated meteorology. It makes you wonder whether the cloud was ever really there or whether it was a product of our need for miracles.

Smilde's art-historical references include seventeenth-century landscape painting, but also hint at symbols of fertility and the imminence of nature. The locations in which the artist situates the clouds play an important role in their interpretation. In a church they look celestial, against the backdrop of a psychiatric hospital they take on a cinematic quality, and floating down a museum hallway they become both artefacts and proof of man's imagination and resourcefulness.

Louise O. Fresco

TO FEED A GROWING WORLD, WE NEED TO CHANGE OUR SYSTEMS, OUR VALUES

Countries all over the world increasingly face ecological and societal pressure attributable to global patterns of unsustainable production and consumption. Climate, pandemics, biodiversity, migration – the world crises seem to accumulate. Even if objectively, there always have been crises, they are now often interconnected and affect more people than ever before. It may seem like a Gordian knot, but that does not mean there is one brilliant stroke that offers a total

Louise O. Fresco

FOOD-WATER-ENERGY NEXUS

Because there is not one food system, but tens of thousands of food systems worldwide, solutions are diverse. Producing and consuming food may be location-specific and embedded in culture and tradition, but can also involve worldwide networks and major volumes of trade. Agriculture is one of the major consumers of water, although that water may remain available locally if not polluted. Agriculture and food processing, transport and retailing together are major consumers of energy. Solutions for a more productive and sustainable agriculture involve optimizing water and energy use. Complex transition processes are partly already underway, but are required everywhere to ensure circular and resource efficient food systems that provide the healthy food that billions of people need for their wellbeing. Food, water, energy, as well as human, animal and ecosystem health are public goods. Together, they depend on natural resources, trade regimes, competition for foreign direct investments, international research and innovation, and many more factors that need national and international agreements.

SYSTEMS

System thinking has gained prominence in the agriculture and food sector and is now commonplace. Most food-insecure people live in areas characterized by political and economic instability and severe poverty. Even in high income countries the disadvantaged households are most vulnerable to an unhealthy diet. Because food is an integral part of culture and so closely linked with tradition, values and emotions, solutions to

food system failures are subject to intense debate and controversy. Notwithstanding solid scientific advancement on issues like fertilizers, genetic improvement and animal welfare, polarization, confusion and uncertainty about facts abound. Sometimes this is caused by differences in methodologies, sometimes it is still a result of scientific uncertainty, trade-offs or the growing understanding of evolving issues. This is particularly true of the contribution of agriculture and food to greenhouse gas emissions.

GLOBAL GOVERNANCE

Public confidence in science-based solutions is declining in many countries, if not everywhere, with different interest groups taking a pick 'n' mix approach to science, choosing the facts and arguments that suit them best. This results in a lack of trust and disagreement about the best way forward. Achieving solutions for food systems must go hand-in-hand with achieving other sustainable development goals (SDGs) and therefore requires new thinking about the governance of agriculture and food systems. Roundtables and dialogues are required that connect governments, civil society (including NGOs and consumer organizations) and private enterprises (including farmers) with scientists. The only way to move people forward is to gain mutual trust and develop common values. Creating a science-policy interface and developing local, national and international agendas to ultimately provide enough safe, nutritious, affordable and sustainable food, water and energy for everyone is of the utmost importance.

Achieving solutions for food systems must go hand-in-hand with achieving other sustainable development goals (SDGs) and therefore requires new thinking about the governance of agriculture and food systems.

Prof. Dr. Louise O. Fresco, agriculture and food expert, is chairperson of the Executive Board of Wageningen University & Research. From 2006 to July 2014, she was a professor at the University of Amsterdam. Before that, she was the Assistant Director-General of FAO, the Food and Agriculture Organization of the United Nations in Rome.

Mogu

ART BOOSTS INNOVATION

Mogu brings nature closer to people, developing solutions derived from using mycelium as part of bio-fabrication-based processes. Its certified products are plastic free and have the lowest possible environmental impact.

According to recent research published by construction blog BIMhow, the international construction sector is responsible for 23 per cent of air pollution, 50 per cent of climate change, 40 per cent of drinking water pollution and 50 per cent of landfill waste. Obviously, construction is harmful to the environment as well as human living conditions. To tackle such urgent issues, Mogu develops alternative production processes and products for interior architecture that can positively inform the way we build. Mogu underwrites a paradigm in which humans work with nature, rather than against it.

The technology underlying Mogu's products is based on mycelium, the vegetative stage of mushrooms. Over the years, Mogu has developed protocols to monitor the growth of these organisms on pre-engineered substrates that consist of low-value, agro-industrial materials, such as upcycled textile residues. The methods use very limited energy, yet result in technically sound, aesthetically pleasing, stable, safe, durable and biodegradable products.

Mogu has supplied both floor and acoustic tiles to greatly improve the comfort of the Netherlands Pavilion at Expo 2020 Dubai. Thanks to the natural production process, every tile has a unique, intriguingly aesthetic surface that brings life to otherwise dull, mass-produced surfaces and indoor spaces. For the Netherlands Pavilion, Mogu has produced and supplied customised acoustic modular products bearing the Expo 2020 Dubai logo.

Mogu's products are the result of close collaboration between humans and nature. Nature's inherent intelligence and adaptability is coupled with man's creative power to disrupt the design of everyday products. Mogu's natural, sustainable interior products point the way to inclusive, truly responsible, non-pollutive production practices that can contribute to a healthier planet.

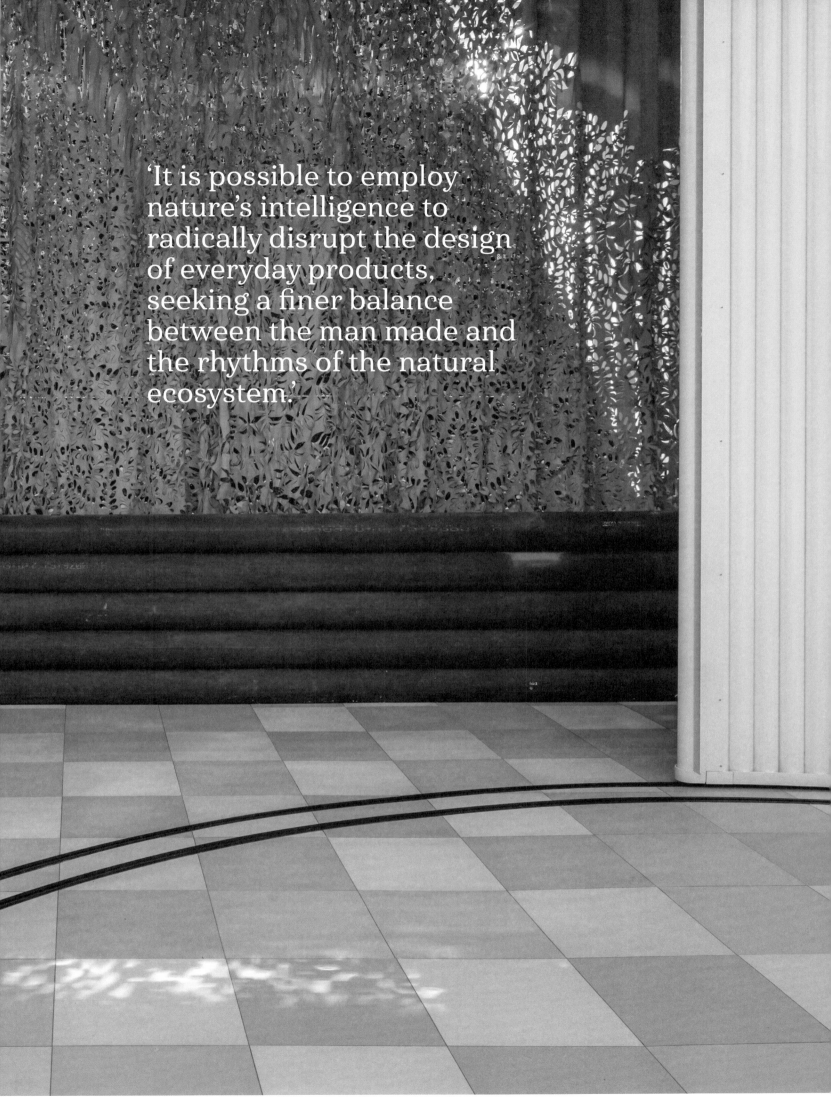

'It is possible to employ nature's intelligence to radically disrupt the design of everyday products, seeking a finer balance between the man made and the rhythms of the natural ecosystem.'

Kadir van Lohuizen

**ART BOOSTS
INNOVATION**

'The question is not whether sea levels will rise by one, two or three metres, but when.'

Kadir van Lohuizen documents the impact of human activity on our planet and its climate. Innovative methods of food production methods can either provide part of the solution or exacerbate the problems.

Soviet scientists appear to have used the term Anthropocene back in the 1960s. Ecologist Eugene Stoermer is widely credited with introducing it in the West, where it was popularized in 2000 by atmospheric chemist Paul Crutzen. Although not officially recognized as a geological era, the Anthropocene is a suitable descriptor for the last century or so, in which human activity – industry, mining, logging, construction and transport – has permanently and noticeably altered the Earth's surface, ecology and even climate. The effects of the climate crisis are the subject of Kadir van Lohuizen's photo series *Rising Tide*. Van Lohuizen travelled to Greenland, Miami, New York, Kiribati, the Marshall Islands, Fiji, Jakarta, Bangladesh, Papua New Guinea, Panama and the UK to talk to and portray coastal dwellers, as well as the policymakers trying to protect their living environment. *Rising Tide* presents the

human stories behind the data on melting ice sheets, salinization of agricultural land and disappearing islands.

Covid-19 travel restrictions forced Van Lohuizen to stay closer to home for his most recent project. It focuses on food production in the Netherlands, which, despite its modest size and high population density, is the world's second largest agricultural exporter. Dutch agriculture is heavily automated and industrialized. Zero-grazing livestock farming, vertical vegetable cultivation, aquaponic fish farming and other innovations have greatly increased the yield per hectare. However, these industrial production methods also have ecological and public health drawbacks. The recent zoonotic pandemic has really driven home the disastrous effects of human interference on ecology. This is why Van Lohuizen, who started out reporting on civil wars and other armed conflicts, has concentrated on environmental issues in recent years. It's not a war between humans that will be the end of us, but rather the war between humans and nature.

Atelier van Lieshout

ART BOOSTS INNOVATION

'Like death, time is one of life's certainties. It will always move on.'

Atelier Van Lieshout presents a contemporary memento mori, which doubles as humanity's alarm clock. The crushing wheels of time either count down to destruction or welcome a new dawn.

There is only one certainty in life: the passage of time and the inevitability of death. The series of clocks by Atelier Van Lieshout (AVL) reminds us of that. In the face of this sobering truism, they imply the end of time itself or at least the conclusion of our current era and its destructive dynamics.

On a personal level, time can feel highly variable. Hours can feel like weeks or months, while some days seem to fly by in a matter of minutes. The digitization of our world has greatly increased the perceived elasticity of time. Our computers transport us from the here and now to other locations and time zones. AVL's *Seven Digit Clock* aptly illustrates this brand of virtual time travel by randomly displaying past and future dates and times. The *Back to the Future Clock* is a more

traditional, analogue timepiece, but its arms frequently slow down, speed up or change direction in a bewildering choreography of non-linear time. The *Down the Drain Clock* appears even more archaic. The massive hourglass looks like it will take hours to run out, but it expends itself in a few seconds after it has been upended.

Time, history and the future are a common thread in AVL's body of work. The series of sculptures and installations were inspired by past civilizations and ideologies, from prehistoric cavemen and the first sedentary communities to the technology-worshipping Futurists of the early twentieth century. They present alternative ways of working, producing and living, but never in an unambiguously utopian manner; there is always an underlying dark side. This also holds true for the clocks. They might release us from the tyranny of time, but they also signal our possible extinction. Then again, they could also be perceived as a call to action.

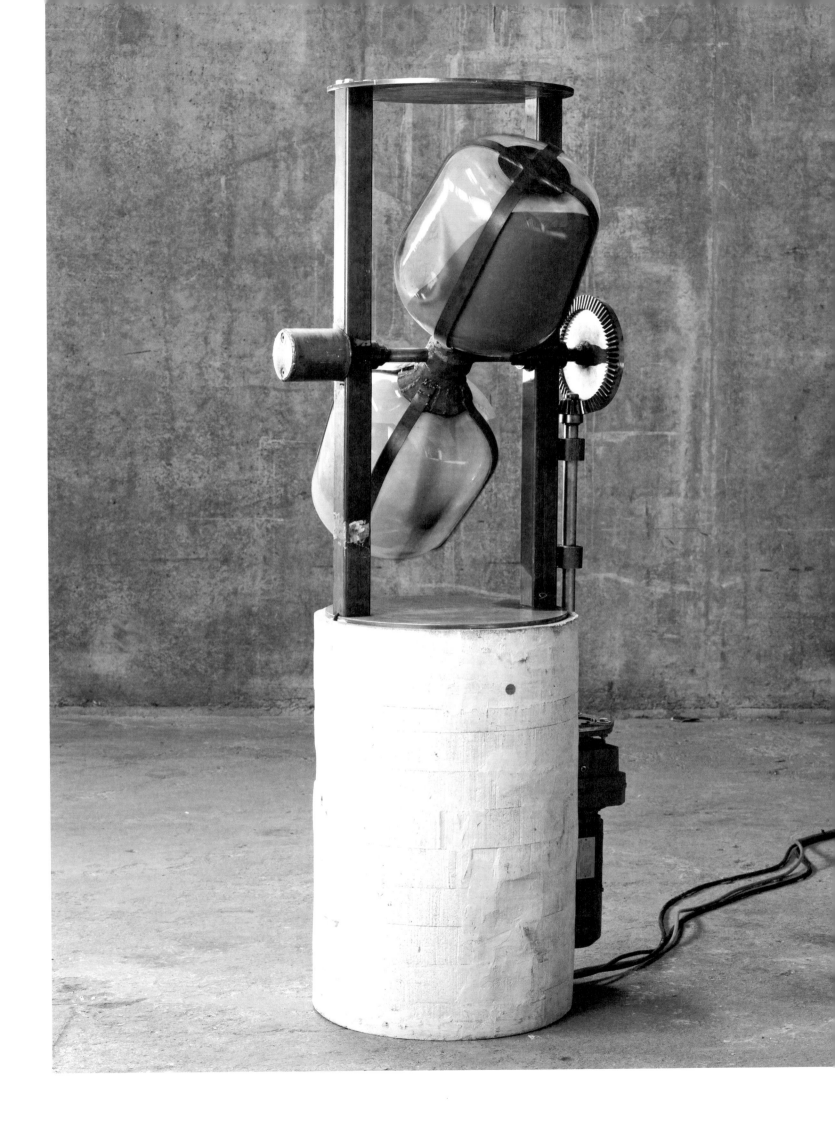

The clock is running down when it comes to climate control on the planet. Time is slowly ticking away. That is the warning given by Joep van Lieshout's clocks. They seem to be on a collision course, with one clock ticking away to the moment of destruction, the other forward to a new dawn.

Marjan van Aubel's foil is an aesthetic and technical implementation of the classic solar panel. It allows filtered light to fall on the 'food mountain' in which asparagus, tomatoes and herbs come to life.

Studio Roosegaarde

ART BOOSTS INNOVATION

'Let's be the architects of our new normal and create better places to meet and interact.'

Sustainable agriculture can be greatly enhanced using light recipes. Studio Roosegaarde's GROW uses LED lighting to stimulate crop growth and thus reduce the need for pesticides.

According to the United Nations there will be 9 billion people on earth in the year 2050. We won't be able to produce enough food to feed all those mouths using existing agricultural methods and techniques, at least not sustainably. Following the green revolution of the 1950s and 1960s, which boosted food production using agrochemicals, it's time for the next step. GROW by Studio Roosegaarde points the way.

The GROW project takes the artificial lighting used in greenhouses and vertical farming and applies it outdoors. Special LED lights that run on solar batteries beam red and blue light onto crops, mixed with invisible UV radiation. These light recipes induce growth and reduce the need for pesticides by up to 50 per cent.

GROW is the result of a two-year, self-initiated research project undertaken by Studio Roosegaarde in collaboration with plant biologists. Theories as well as prototypes were tested extensively using a 20,000 m² field of leeks. The precision lighting has been fine-tuned to short intervals to reduce the light pollution associated with traditional greenhouse farming.

GROW is a quintessential Studio Roosegaarde initiative. The Rotterdam-based studio combines science and design to tackle today's urgent problems and improve urban life. The results can be described as 'technological poetry'. Studio Roosegaarde's body of work includes a *Smog Free Tower*, a huge vacuum cleaner that creates clean-air parks. There is also the long-running *Smart Highway* that could potentially replace energy-consuming street lights thanks to a light absorbent road coating that glows in the dark.

Daan Roosegaarde, the studio's founder, describes today's designers as 'hippies with a business plan, who dream and build in order to make the world a better place'. GROW is an addition to the existing agricultural toolbox and will hopefully enable humanity to keep producing sufficient food.

Buro Belén

ART BOOSTS INNOVATION

Buro Belén finds new ways to protect our bodies from the harmful effects of sunlight using bioplastics that don't block the production of vitamin D and have a zero-carbon footprint.

The sun is our biggest source of energy and the basis for life on earth. But you can have too much of a good thing. Over the centuries people have found ways to protect their skin from harmful UV light and sunburn. But clothes that cover us not only block the piercing rays of the sun, but also prevent the production of the vitamin D that we so desperately need. Sunblock manufactured using chemicals is mostly oil based and, in the long run, harms our bodies and the environment. Since 2018, Brecht Duijf and Lenneke Langenhuijsen of Buro Belén have been searching for alternatives that are both safe and sustainable. Their self-initiated research project Sun+ includes Unseen Sunglasses cut from thin sheets of metal which only let in a third of the sunlight and Sun Veils, ultra-light garments that envelop the body.

Buro Belén has developed two products for the Netherlands Pavilion at Expo 2020 Dubai. The first is a curtain measuring 44 by 14 metres that elegantly surrounds the VIP area. The curtain, which is soft to the touch and warm to the eye, features laser-cut images of mangroves, oleanders, date palms and moringa – Dubai's indigenous vegetation and the basis of its fossil fuel deposits. The bioplastic used, however, has a zero-carbon footprint.

For the pavilion's entrance Buro Belén has designed a canopy that is 11 metres wide and 15 metres long. The biotextile used, which was newly developed in collaboration with Senbis Polymer Innovations and Schmitz Textiles, keeps out harmful UV rays, while enabling sufficient vitamin D production. Whereas conventional polyester sunscreens start deteriorating as soon as the sun hits them, this canopy is long lasting and fully sustainable – an architectural addition perfectly suited to Dubai's sunny climate.

'We believe that everything is interconnected, and we study how the transient nature of this interconnectedness brings new insights and aesthetic materializations that are accessible to everyone.'

Dirk Sijmons
WET-BULB TEMPERATURE AND NAP

Dirk Sijmons (1949) studied architecture at Delft University of Technology and is one of the three founders of H+N+S Landscape Architects. Sijmons received the Rotterdam Maaskant Prize in 2002. In 2004, he was appointed Government Advisor on Landscape by the Ministery of Agriculture, Nature and Food Quality.

This June, in the desert town of Sweihan, situated between Abu Dhabi and Dubai, the temperature hit 51.8°C, the country's record high temperature for that month ... and the warmest part of the year is yet to come. Is the phenomenon of the prolonged scorching heatwave of July and August 2015 repeating itself? That year the Middle East was trapped under what meteorologists call a 'heat dome'. A self-reinforcing process in which hot air rises but is pushed back by a stable high pressure area in the higher atmosphere, warming up even more when it gets back to the surface.

Recently, this phenomenon has also occurred at improbably northern latitudes: in North-west Canada in 2021, Siberia in 2020 and in Europe in 2019. Currently, the Gulf states have to deal with extremely high temperatures almost every year. In 2015, seawater temperatures were measured in the Gulf at 34°C and for weeks the air temperatures ranged from 48°C to 51°C. Combined with the humidity, it was only a few tenths of a degree away from the dreaded 'wet-bulb temperature' of 35°C – the critical combined threshold of temperature and humidity above which people, no matter how much they sweat,

can no longer lose their heat and soon die if they do not find external cooling. Just as we in the Netherlands need the 'NAP' (New Ordnance Datum) as a fixed benchmark in our dynamic delta, the WBT (wet-bulb temperature of a thermometer placed in a wet sock in the wind) is a gauge in a desert climate.

Dubai is like a time machine. The city offers a glimpse of the future environment in the hottest parts of the world if rapid global warming is not halted. It will be a highly regulated existence, where air conditioning is not praised in terms of comfort, but is literally the only way to survive during heatwaves. All of the buildings of Dubai's impressive skyline have to be cooled, sometimes up to 30°C lower than the surrounding temperature. If you realize that cooling takes much more energy than heating, you understand how energy-intensive this desert city is. Life in the houses, the offices, the cars, the huge shopping malls, the leisure facilities – including indoor ski slopes – takes place entirely in enclosed, air-conditioned spaces. A kind of hugely roofed-in social-spatial experiment to survive in an increasingly inhospitable climate. A scaled-up Biosphere 2, were it not for the fact that this urban region is just about the opposite of the autarky pursued by the 1991-1993 experiment in the Arizona desert, where six people locked themselves in a giant self-supportive greenhouse. In the UAE all conceivable products and foodstuffs are flown in via – also air-conditioned – air transport, the giant airport is the hub of a successful luxury airline that spins a worldwide web of business and tourist connections that provide an influx of new investments and new blood.

Is Dubai a modernist triumph over seemingly impossible natural conditions? Or is it the

pinnacle of what one might call 'fossil expressionism': a world made possible only by the tailwind of vast oil wealth and that can only survive thanks to the daily deployment of a humongous amount of energy. Dubai is certainly an example of the solutionist fyke-tech lock-in steps that shows how difficult it will be to reverse our course in the light of the climate crisis. Its government saw the oil age ending, thought up a strategy to switch to a service economy, and, having the funds to back that up, became the safe trading spot in the Middle East and the hub to Asia. Confronted with the climate change, the country doesn't want to risk this position, let alone its zillion-dollar real estate investments, and voilà a technical solution to counter the side-effects of earlier choices presents itself. As I write this text, the UAE took the historic step of seeding the clouds with silver-iodide and flashing electric charges into the clouds with drones, forcing a refreshing rain to fall on the scorching city. It worked and showed that the law that geographical conditions dictate whether a settlement can be successful can be inverted. Victorious mankind shows that the climate conditions to be changed to make a settlement successful. Warnings were ignored that geoengineering might very well cause side-effects. Regionally, if it rains on Dubai, it immediately means that ecosystems and people living somewhere else where it would have rained will no longer get this rain – a recipe for conflict. Or, on a larger scale, which is not inconceivable, there could be a sorcerer's apprentice effect, disrupting the entire planet's climate even further.

The Netherlands pavilion is an interesting attempt to develop a low-tech perspective to surviving in this environment. Quite rightly the designers chose the nexus between energy, water, and food as their environmental battlefield. All three can be related to one another

Tomorrow, we are all brothers and sisters.

and even be expressed in one another's units and show a waterbed effect. Solving one of the three will most likely result in problems popping up in one of the others. The pavilion shows that there are ways to evade that waterbed effect by decreasing the turnover speed of the whole triad. This is done by reviving the tacit knowledge of Bedouins, with their Barjeel tents with air vents ingeniously cooling the interior. And by harvesting the morning dew from the air and using this small amount of precipitation for food production. The little bit of energy needed to fuel the processes is generated by solar cells bathing in the abundant sunlight. Scaling up and integrating these traditional techniques with high-tech energy systems is perhaps the most promising way forward. The question is,

of course: Can this 'Biosphere 3 experiment' be scaled up?

But who are we to moralistically rub these proud desert dwellers' noses in their vulnerable position? Wouldn't continuing to build well below sea level, like we do, elicit similar comments of disbelief from their side? Didn't we earn our wealth from fossil fuels too, the gas profits partly financing our expensive system of water safety defence? Do we both represent some kind of heroism on a lost post? Who is to say if one of the two is going to end up as a Fehlsiedlung, as German historical geographers characterize abandoned settlements? Only the climate-disrupted future will tell. There's going to be a lengthy struggle to hold both positions, that's for sure. In this future, we're all brothers and sisters.

Marjan van Aubel

ART BOOSTS INNOVATION

'One hour of sunlight is enough to supply the entire planet with energy for a year. It's about time we start using this untapped potential.'

Marjan van Aubel's third-generation solar cells combine functionality with sustainability and beauty. They generate energy, but also create a subtle light show.

Solar technology has been around longer than you may think. The earliest examples of solar panels date back to the beginning of the nineteenth century. Since then major advances have been made, especially over the past few decades. In 2020, there were at least 37 countries around the world with the capacity to produce over one gigawatt of solar-powered electricity.

Despite this, solar technology still lacks something, in the view of Marjan van Aubel. The almost exclusive focus on high efficiency, low cost and mass production has led to standardized solutions and a lack of attention being paid to alternatives. Van Aubel therefore prefers to speak of 'solar design' and seeks to infuse technology with aesthetics and emotion. Her Current Table, for example, gathers energy like a photosynthesising plant and allows you to recharge your devices by plugging into it. And the recent Sunne is a solar-powered indoor light that imitates the sun.

At the Netherlands Pavilion Marjan van Aubel covered the skylights with transparent solar cells. They collect energy from the sun in Dubai to provide power. At the same time, they allow sunlight into the space, filtering the correct spectrum of light for the edible plants growing indoors. The design consisting of lines and patterns creates a playful moiré effect of reflections on the walls and floor. Functionality and beauty go hand in hand. These solar cells of the future are made of coloured organic photovoltaic material (OPV), which is non-toxic. They are printed on PET and produced in a circular manner. Because of their light weight they are easy to transport and install. Moreover, they can be easily disassembled and reassembled. This solar panelled roof will be repurposed after Expo 2020 Dubai.

Theo Jansen

ART BOOSTS INNOVATION

Theo Jansen has created a whole new species using nothing but plastic tubing, wind and his own imagination. His *Strandbeesten* evolve into low-tech entities with rudimentary brains and survival skills.

Theo Jansen is a creator in the most fundamental sense of the word. For over 30 years he has been building generations of a new species that will eventually survive their creator and continue to evolve on their own. Yet his creatures don't involve multi-million-dollar machines or mindboggling genesplicing technology. Jansen builds his skeletons from yellow plastic tubes held together with tape and rope. Every new generation incorporates lessons learned from its predecessors and is tested on the beach of Jansen's native The Hague. Hence their name: *Strandbeesten*: beach beasts.

Jansen studied applied physics, but before graduating, he changed direction and decided to become an artist instead. To him, art and science are not separate worlds, but rather two related ways of applying imagination and creativity to natural laws and phenomena. He started working on his

Strandbeesten after creating a flying saucer and a painting machine.

Rather than use wheels, these creatures rely on the mechanical movement of legs and joints. They move sideways like crabs or imitate the undulating progress of caterpillars. Sails catch the wind, which serves as an energy source. The *Umerus* (2009) introduced a propulsion system in the shoulders. Since the *Calceamente* (2014) all *Strandbeesten* have large feet that enable them to navigate rough surfaces. Recent generations have also learned to float so as not to get bogged down in sand.

In the meantime, Jansen has also developed a system to store wind energy and a piston-driven neural system that basically constitutes a rudimentary brain. As opposed to the black box of digital technology – usually associated with artificial intelligence – the whole mechanism operates in plain sight and is much sturdier. NASA has recently asked Jansen to think about a low-tech reconnaissance robot for their upcoming mission to Venus. That would make a *Strandbeest* the first earthling to set foot on the planet.

'The wall between art and
engineering exists only in our minds.'

Eef de Graaf

ART BOOSTS INNOVATION

Documentary filmmaker Eef de Graaf took stock of the Netherlands' testing grounds for the transition to a sustainable society: innovation driven by an increasing sense of urgency.

The Netherlands' National Climate Agreement, which was signed in 2019, boasts ambitious targets: at least a 49 per cent reduction in CO_2 emissions in comparison with 1990 by 2030, and a 95 per cent reduction by the year 2050. However, alongside political determination, practical projects will be required to achieve these goals. This means finding new, sustainable ways to produce energy and food. The industrial cycle needs to be closed, and waste must be eliminated. And all this has to be achieved in a natural environment increasingly dominated by rising sea levels, subsiding land and salinization of farmland.

In the years leading up to the National Climate Agreement, documentary filmmaker Eef de Graaf explored the outer edges of the Dutch delta, from Zeeland in the southwest to the Wadden Islands in the northeast. In *Sustainable Islands* she talks to scientists, entrepreneurs, policymakers and concerned citizens struggling with water management challenges, experimenting with new food crops, transitioning to renewable energy and trying to combine necessary consumption with environmental restraint. They live and work on the many islands along the coast that function as both testing grounds and showcases for innovative projects. However, for De Graaf, these islands are also a metaphor for the individual efforts that desperately need to be connected, combined and scaled up in order to truly have an impact.

De Graaf originally trained as a figurative painter, and a certain visual sensitivity shines through in her documentary. She portrays Dutch landscapes the way Ruysdael, Van Goyen and other Old Masters did, focusing on the man-made landscapes under vast, cloudy skies. Unlike her predecessors, she is fully aware of the fact that this landscape is only 'on loan'. During her period of filming the Netherlands experienced two of its hottest and driest summers ever, driving home the urgency of change.

People tend to think in terms of neatly parcelled projects, but in the climate crisis everything is connected.

Marie-Thérèse van Thoor

THE STORY OF WATER. THE DUTCH LEGACY AT WORLD EXPOS

Marie-Thérèse van Thoor (PhD) is associate professor at the Faculty of Architecture and the Built Environment of Delft University of Technology. She is trained as an architecture historian, and is theoretically and practically experienced in the field of Heritage and Architecture. She has published and edited several books and an academic journal.

Connecting Minds, Creating the Future, the central theme of the Expo 2020 Dubai, is divided into three subthemes, Opportunity, Mobility and Sustainability. In line with the last subtheme, the Dutch organization has chosen the motto Uniting Water, Energy & Food for its entry. However, the Netherlands pavilion is more than just a theme building: it's a materialized sensory experience of the nexus water – energy – food. It literally connects water, energy and food and presents its message in such a way that the visitor sees, hears, smells, tastes and feels it. According to V8 Architects, this is what sets the pavilion apart from other pavilions: 'The pavilion is the exhibition and user experience.'

The design, by a consortium including Expomobilia, V8 Architects, Kossmanndejong and Witteveen+Bos, is a unique biotope of circularity and sustainability. With its unique and innovative execution of a representation of a typically Dutch theme, this biotope is in line with a trend that began with the Netherland pavilion at Expo 58 in Brussels. At the time, a team of architects – 'architectengroep brussel '58, boks, van den broek-bakema, rietveld' – presented the theme, The Water as Enemy and Ally of the Dutch People, in a very special way. For the first time, the entire Dutch presentation was dominated by one theme, and for the first time, the architecture of the pavilion itself was part of it.

Although from early on World Expos commemorated important events such as the centenary of the French Revolution (Paris, 1889) or the completion of the Panama Canal (San Francisco, 1915), the introduction of a theme or focal point only became more common from 1925 onwards. In that year the Exposition Internationale des Arts Décoratifs et Industriels Modernes in Paris specifically focused on, as its name suggests, modern decorative and industrial arts in the broadest sense of the word. But this exhibition was an exception; its contributions were more about various (sub)categories of the arts than about country presentations. From the beginning, the intentions of most World Expos hardly deviated from the intention of the 1851 Great Exhibition of the Works of Industry of all Nations in London: 'To forward the progress of industrial civilization.' Word Expos – called exhibitions, expositions or fairs depending on the language – became the stages on which countries could show their biggest and best, often technical innovations. In addition, they offered countries from all over the world the opportunity to promote their typical or country-specific products. For the London Exhibition of 1851, Joseph Paxton designed the famous Crystal Palace. This immense hall brought all exhibitors and countries together under one roof. Depending on the size of their entries, a small or large part of the hall was available for this purpose. The Dutch entry was modest. In a bay, separated by partitions and cloth sheets, there were cupboards and display cases filled with household goods and handicrafts.

The first World Expo was held in London, in 1851. For this, Joseph Paxton designed the famous Crystal Palace, which housed the entries of all countries. All exhibitors were given the opportunity to showcase their best, technical innovations, or to praise their typical products.

After the World Expo ended, the Crystal Palace was rebuilt in Sydenham, where it served as a space for exhibitions and events until 1936.

The concept of a large, temporary exhibition hall proved so functional that it was impossible to imagine a World Expo without one for a long time. However, the exhibits were very diverse. They ranged from jewellery and fragile crockery to heavy and noisy machinery, with livestock and innovative agriculture also being on display. In addition, the programme would include entertainment and festivities. This is why, from 1855 onwards, Word Expos increasingly included a second or third large hall; some World Expos occasioned the realization of exhibition spaces that were given a permanent function after the event.

In Paris in 1867, various small buildings and so-called follies arose around the main hall. They complemented the exhibition in the main hall and exemplified model homes, workshops or farms. They showed specific products or production processes and represented styles, constructions or building types. They may have included a Dutch dairy farm, a Turkish coffee house or a Swiss chalet, but they were not country pavilions in the usual sense of the word, that is, buildings in which participating countries showed their entries and products. Country pavilions appeared at the 1900 Exposition Universelle in Paris. Along the Seine, various countries built pavilions in a characteristic, often picturesque, national style and together these constituted the so-called Rue des Nations. In that year, the Dutch contribution was limited to an exhibition in one of the large halls. It was not until the 1910 Exposition Universelle et Internationale in Brussels that the Netherlands first built a country pavilion.

From 1900 onwards, it was impossible to imagine World Expos without country pavilions. Many of these became the architectural calling cards of the participating countries.

In the twentieth century, the World Expos themselves no longer exclusively focused on progress. In the words of John E. Findling: 'Fairs have come to exhibit comparative national life-styles rather than simply industrial progress.' In the first decades of the twentieth century, the focus on themes was sometimes also reflected in the names, for example Exposition Internationale Coloniale, Maritime et d'Art Flamand for the Word Expo held in Antwerp in 1930. The Netherlands pavilion, designed by architect H.Th. Wijdeveld, focused on the second subtheme, featuring impressive models of lock complexes and the port of Rotterdam. Water proved an excellent theme for expressing the Dutch lifestyle or identity. The first World Expo after the Second World War, the Brussels Exposition Universelle et Internationale, or Expo 58 for short, was optimistic and full of expectation. It's slogan was: Balance sheet of the world for a more humane world. Technology at the service of humankind. Progress for humankind through the progress of technology. The Expo centred on the Atomium, a 150 billion-time magnification of an iron crystal in the centre of the grounds that represented the progress of technology. Rather than a country pavilion, the Atomium was a theme pavilion, in line with the tradition of nineteenth-century follies and spectacular eye-catchers such as the Eiffel Tower.

The eye-catcher of the 1889 Paris World Expo was the Eiffel Tower. It would become the icon of the city.

For the 1900 Expo, several countries built a pavilion in a characteristic, national style in the so-called Rue des Nations on the Seine bank. From then on, it was impossible to imagine World Expos without country pavilions.

Among the country pavilions in Brussels, the Dutch entry attracted a lot of attention. The pavilion, which was actually a pavilion complex, focused on the relationship of the Dutch people with water. Water was also literally the connecting element of the entire presentation. The Dutch complex featured four connected buildings surrounded by a Dutch (water) landscape that included hydraulic elements and polder land. Amid the buildings and central in the landscape was a dike topped by a lighthouse. On the lower side of the dike was the polder land, with a polder drainage ditch. A screw pump pumped water from this ditch into a higher water basin on the other side of the dike. The installation constituted a permanent, live demonstration of the draining of wet polder land. Inside the buildings, the Dutch theme was represented in more detail by various complementary exhibits. These included scale models of the Zuiderzee and Delta Works and allowed the visitors, settled on deckchairs arranged on a life-size replica of a ship, to pretend they were actually on a sea voyage. Sheep and a goat grazed in the polder grass and at the far end, the complex was closed off by an agricultural pavilion. This was a wooden, thatched building that was partly recycled after the World Expo. Its parts were reused in the Limburg municipality of Bunde, as was the wooden mooring post that was the logo of the Dutch entry.

Next to the Dutch pavilion, the Philips corporation built its own 'pavilion of the future', an iconic, hyperbolic-paraboloid construction for a multimedia experience of light, sound, colour and rhythm called the Poème Électronique. Initially, Gerrit Rietveld's name had circulated for the design of this pavilion – Rietveld had by then been focusing on the relationship between sensory experience and architecture for many years – but the Philips Pavilion was ultimately the result of a collaboration between Le Corbusier, Iannis Xenakis and Edgar Varèse. Multimedia presentations subsequently became trending topics. For the Expo 70 in Osaka, Jaap Bakema and Carel Weeber designed a Dutch pavilion comprising a number of stacked containers in which films could be projected, truly a viewing machine. And the live experience of Dutch landscapes proved successful as well. The theme of the Dutch pavilion for the Expo 2000 in Hannover was Holland Creates Space. Inside the pavilion, designed by MVRDV, various types of Dutch landscapes were literally stacked on top of each other. This showed how innovative our country was in creating space and cultivating nature.

Since 1958, the Netherlands has demonstrated that a pavilion can not only serve as a space for displaying Dutch products or function as a representation of a theme, but that it is also a unique materialization of the 'product the Netherlands'.

Marie-Thérèse van Thoor

Birthe Leemeijer

ART BOOSTS INNOVATION

Birthe Leemeijer searched for the essence of one of the oldest polders in the Netherlands and came up with a perfume. L'Essence de Mastenbroek triggers both memory and imagination.

The nose is an important, yet often underappreciated sensory organ. It helps us identify and better appreciate food, and warns us of dangers, like fire or poison. But it also triggers our memory on an emotional level that far surpasses what a photograph or audio recording can provoke. Scent has the power to transport us to a time and place beyond images and words.

L'Essence de Mastenbroek (2005) is a perfume evoking Mastenbroek, a polder that dates back to the fourteenth century, making it one of the oldest tracts of reclaimed land in the Netherlands. Nowadays the landscape is hemmed in by urban expansion. Artist Birthe Leemeijer decided to capture the essence of Mastenbroek before it's too late. To help select the perfume's ingredients she brought together a group of locals, mostly livestock farmers from families that have lived and worked in the area for centuries, and started a collaboration with perfumer Alessandro Gualtieri. L'Essence de Mastenbroek has high notes of grass and hay, fresh milk in the middle and bovine notes in the lower register.

After its introduction in 2005, the perfume was sold worldwide, attesting to an appeal that transcends local sensitivity. In 2012 Leemeijer handed over production and distribution to local residents. They installed a fountain in the foundations of an abandoned farm, where owners of an original flask can get an annual refill. For the Expo 2020 Dubai, the source in Mastenbroek will be connected to the Netherlands pavilion by means of an underground glass pipeline.

L'Essence de Mastenbroek is typical of Leemeijer's work, which seeks to change our perception and experience of the natural environment. She had used scent before in *Dreamscapes* (2003), where she administered aromatic substances to arboretum visitors as a way of sparking their imaginations. L'Essence de Mastenbroek takes things one step further. It evokes a specific history and identity, but leaves room for other landscapes and memories.

'By creating connections and entering unexpected relationships, I want to challenge preconceived notions and disrupt how we think about space.'

Vilma Henkelman

ART BOOSTS INNOVATION

Vilma Henkelman's ceramics are an exploration of life in clay. They are about connecting with the world's most basic material and being in the moment.

Of all artistic media, pottery is the most down to earth, literally. Wet clay – traditionally moulded by hand – is shaped into utilitarian objects, often vessels used to prepare or store food: containers made of earth, holding what the earth brought forth.

For Vilma Henkelman, making ceramics is about communing directly with the earth. In an interview she once even simply stated: 'I am clay.' At the pottery wheel she exerts concentrated pressure on the material with her hands and sometimes her entire body. It's direct, physical work that results in organically powerful forms. They bear no trace of hesitation or doubt. They are perfect without being flawless in the mechanical sense of the word.

Signing her works all over with the imprint of her thumbs, Henkelman drills down to the essence of the primordial matter. She often refrains from using glazes, in order to underscore the clay's strength and vitality. Tactility and a certain stillness go hand in hand.

Henkelman opened her own studio in 1969, and for the first few years she focused on functional objects like pots and vases – mostly sturdy and timeless pieces with a minimum of ornamentation. Later, she enlarged these shapes to monumental dimensions, often as big as a person, and over time these transformed into autonomous sculptures. In recent years she has come full circle and has returned to the ceramic archetypes of her early days, the Japanese tea bowl, or chawan, being one of her favourites.

The work on display at the Expo 2020 Dubai dates from Henkelman's formative period in the late 1970s and early 1980s. In it she boldly explores extremes in shape and material processing, finding freedom in the limitations of her medium of choice.

'The beauty of imperfection is born from being in harmony with the natural and unsophisticated, a simplicity and spontaneity coming directly from within.'

The Netherla

nds

هولندا

nds

The Netherlands participation for Expo 2020 Dubai has been made possible by:

PARTNERS
Van Oord
Shell

SPONSORS
Ahrend
Bavaria
Blue Box
Bom Groep
Fourleaf
Holland Water
Hoogendoorn
Impriva
Keller Kitchens
Koppert Biological Systems
Leadax
LeasePlan
Lensvelt
MJ Tech
Meever & Meever
Prakash Trading Company
Priva
Ryberg
Signify
Schijvens
The Vegetarian Butcher
Quooker

SUPPLIERS
Consortium Building
V8 Architects
ExpoMobilia
Witteveen+Bos
Kossmandejong / BIND

Specialist Consultants
SIGN
Aardlab

Operations
Van der Linde Catering
GL Events
Meetinglinq
Transguard
Wirtz Film & Experience Agency

Innovators
Sunglacier Technologies
(Ap Verheggen)
Marjan van Aubel Studio
Mogu
Buro Belén

PROGRAMMING
Track Renewable Energy
& partners
Track Off Shore Energy & partners
Track Water & partners & partners
Track Horticulture & food
& parters
Track Circular Economy & partners
Taskforce Health Care
Orange Sports Forum
VNO-NCW
NLinBusiness
Municipality of Rotterdam
& Rotterdam partners

ARTISTS
Birthe Leemeijer
Berndnaut Smilde
Daan Roosegaarde
David Middendorp /
Another Kind of Blue
Eef de Graaf
Atelier van Lieshout
Kadir van Lohuizen
Organisation in Design
*(Atelier Boelhouwer, Atelier LVDW,
Beer Holthuis, Chardé Brouwer,
Lionne van Deursen,
Nienke Hoogvliet, Sanne Visser,*
*Shahar Livne, Studio Billie van
Katwijk, Studio Sway,
Tamara Orjola, Thieu Custers
and Pauline Wiersema, Xandra
van der Eijk and Yvon Smeets)*
Studio Makkink & Bey
Theo Jansen
Vilma Henkelman

MUSEUM PARTNERS
Rijksmuseum
National Maritime Museum
Kunstmuseum Den Haag
Mauritshuis
Van Gogh Museum
Museum Panorama Mesdag

GOVERNMENT
Government of the Netherlands
Ministry of Foreign Affairs
Ministry of Education,
Culture & Science
Netherlands Enterprise Agency
Cultural Heritage Agency
of the Netherlands

And many more.

Credits

This publication accompanies the Netherlands Pavilion for Expo 2020 Dubai,
1 October 2021 - 31 March 2022

Concept & Art Direction nicole uniquole
Design Marty Schoutsen, Opera Concept & Design, Breda (NL)
Copy editing D'Laine Camp
Translation In Other Words
Photography Aasiya Jagadeesh: 2/3, 6/7, 8/9, 16, 45, 52/53, 56/57,
58/59, 60/61, 62, 66/67/68/69, 86/87, 92, 94/95, 99, 110/111, 122/123, 124/125, 128,
134/135; V8 Architects: 10/11, 12, 18/19, 23, 24/25, 28/29, 32/33, 38/39, 44, 54/55, 73;
Kossmanndejong: 40, 75, 130/131; Opera: 4/5; Reineke Otten (Buro Belen): 64/65;
Schijvens: 63; Shutterstock: 51; iStock: 78/79; RedCharlie: 83; Noaa Led: 85;
123RF: 103; Getty Images, Hulton Archive: 114; Wikimedia Commons: 117; Expo 2020
Dubai: 101; Marco Zwinkels: 70/71, 107; Ap Verheggen: 77; Berndnaut Smilde: 81;
Kadir van Lohuizen: 89; Atelier van Lieshout: 91; Daan Roosegaarde: 97; Marjan van
Aubel: 105, 132; Eef de Graaf: 108/109; Birthe Leemeijer: 119; Vilma Henkelman: 121.
Printing die Keure, Brugge (Belgium)
Paper 150 grs Munken Polar
Publisher Eelco van Welie, nai010 publishers, Rotterdam (NL)

This publication was made possible by financial support from

nai010 publishers is an internationally orientated publisher specialized in
developing, producing and distributing books in the fields of architecture,
urbanism, art and design. www.nai010.com

nai010 books are available internationally at selected bookstores and from
the following distribution partners:
- North, Central and South America - Artbook | D.A.P., New York, USA,
  dap@dapinc.com
- Rest of the world - Idea Books, Amsterdam, the Netherlands, idea@ideabooks.nl

For general questions, please contact nai010 publishers directly at
sales@nai010.com or visit our website www.nai010.com for further information.

ISBN 978-94-6208-669-2

NUR 648
BISAC ARC024010